Buzzy Pal

Forest Friends

Goofy Giraffe

Just Hangin' Out

Bath Time

Mountain Friends

A Little Visitor

Tim the Tiger

Happy Horse

Ready to splash!

That's a stretch!

In the Garden

"Hello, down there!"

Weekend Ride

Turtle-back Ride

Gardening is fun!

Resting and Nesting

Kyle Koala

Danny Donkey

Garden Days

Jungle Pals

Ribbit!

Snack Time

Delicious Carrots

Time for Dinner

In Flight

Peek-a-boo!

Good morning!

Hello!

Swan Lake

Go bananas!

Turtle Pals

King of the Jungle

Tiger Cub

Prancing Pony

Big, Big Eggs!

Fun in the Sun

On the Pond

Big Baby Chick

Flutter-by Friend

Little Anteater

It's me!

Happy Day

In the Rain Forest

Fluttery Farmer

Fred Fox

"Thanks for the ride!"

Beautiful Bloom

Early Morn

On the Savanna

Cute Caterpillar

Bouncy Pup

Roger Raccoon

In the Backyard

Sunny Spot

Mama is near.

Collecting Flowers

Collecting Honey

Hot Summer Day

Slithery Visitor

Beautiful Wings

Splish Splash